Thank You

Poems by Linzi Garcia

Kansas City   Spartan Press   Missouri

Spartan Press

Kansas City, Missouri

spartanpresskc.com

Spartan
Press

Spartan Press would like to thank Prospero's Books,
The Fellowship of N-finite Jest, The Prospero Institute
of Disquieted P/o/e/t/i/c/s, Will Leathem, Tom Wayne,
Jeanette Powers, j.d.tulloch, Jon Bidwell, Jason Preu,
Mark McClane, Tony Hayden and the whole Osage Arts
Community.

Spew was previously published in *Philosophical Idiot*

CONTENTS

Here's to:

My beautiful family who colored me from the roots up
My favorite cat-lady, world teacher
Our red-headed, prairie-goddess adventurer
My lavender-spawned soul sister
Sun Child and Moon Child
Epic
mH(s), JRB, CC, one r, girasol
New Orleans
All of the strangers who smile with me, bartenders
Librarians, baristas, poets, philosophers
Blues
Dirt
You

Kayla,
You are so lovely!
Your art is beautiful,
& so is your heart!
♡ Imj

Abilene Sunrise

I have never seen
anything more beautiful
than the Kansas plains
kissing the apricot sun
good morning.

To Be a Chapel Construction Worker

The cross scrapes
skies and seemingly out-of-reach
heavens; proving a point?
Debauchery screams otherwise —
I beg to Differ.
Differ is unresponsive.

Growing Up is Weird

Parenting is tiny underwear,
Filling palms with love,
Timelessness gone,
Refined TV time,
Hearts and heads
Heavy and prideful
And eventually gone.
There's a difference
Between childhoods,
Adulthoods,
The hood,
(mama laughs)
Somewhere in between,
Whether naps and spankings
Are punishments
Or rewards.

January 16

i present to you
an entry from a paperweight,
for although the weight of words
is mighty
unfathomable,
there are things
heavier.

Quake Me

I'm not used
                    to Love.
The plates will not
        shake me;
        I will shift with them.

KC Vomit

Cults of ignorance
Make me
Sick to my heart
Puking blood all over
Public restroom toilets
Thinking about beats
And butterflies
And racism
And You.

I'm Not Poet Every Day

When I can't…
        find the right word —
resounds between the walls
of each brain hallway —
a maze where all words
all thoughts are lost
but not worried
        not frightened
for they found god
or a swimming pool
or whatever they drown in
        or fly in —
I. Do. Not. Know.
I cannot Be
receptive on a day
when meat suits slither by
and suck a little more sol.

Hypocrisy Tastes Like a
Honeycomb Feels

Where is the ritual
in Spirituality?
Is it in the way you braid your thoughts,
sip from a selfish and all
providing sun,

                  caress the textures of the day?
Everyday accommodations for the soul
        satisfy Spirit within
                temple, shrine, nest, shell
                without requesting sensations
sent by outside Spirit
dying to be let in.

Me

      little stars
so loud at night
present
a distraction

their presence
only concealed by the soul of reveal
although they're already dead

Monday

some times
I feign the motion of
    ease and delight
for days are scores at a stalemate.

forfeit will not suffice
    so I sacrifice energies
    in the name of accomplishment
    worthy of the day.
we see the sun's questioning gaze.
would it exist
if we did not reflect its intentions?

    I have been told
    when the sun is in the heavens
    the moon cannot sing to us
    yet when the moon is in the heavens
    the sun still hums.

    I will approach
the day with delight
    for even when I cannot dance
the skies and earth will welcome
    life.

Ghost Light Friend

Let us concentrate on realism
playing intimacy of juxtaposed fates.
Chalk lines stain stages
thrust for the majority.

Let us find spaces of refuge
in the name of entertainment —
the sky is the limit,
but we set the height of the sky
with our directors' caps.

Let us experience a world
created only by light and aerials.
Dramatic questions exaggerate
God's knowing it won't work.

Let us give
catwalk heavens, damned organs,
tiptoed curtains.
They invade the play
space of memorized universes,

(time and time)
a gain of fixation.
Criticism hanged him
and he became
our ghost light.

Hide and Seek

We found God in couch cushions,
kissing stray pennies,
resembling Alanis Morissette,
singing like Morgan Freeman.
A men —
a postmodernist at its finest —
possessed and dependent the same,
for we cannot find what we already have,
we can only acknowledge it.
God is wrapped in minty residue,
residing under the weight of beer-coated
thoughts and stained paisley.

first fire

rotating myself —
a marshmallow —
over heat that cooks me golden
and smoke that blinds me rotten

mortality tastes like sushi

we come like water
go like wind
beg like animals
die like You.

when my father was impaled by an aspen

collage of dying leaves
tense throat previously at ease.
'tis the artist who chokes
on photo
synthetic thought.
when roots are bloody,
branches seep red too.
they call it sap;
we call it identity.

Bleh

Everyone is a stranger:
        we still know
Kepler died in misery,
Donovan was a drug addict,
and the *who-knew* girl victimized strangeness
        for entertainment.

Verification of her scars
        (make us wait for transportation)
but when she speaks so sweetly,
stories of her grandchildren cut
sharper than
broken clearance cover-up mirrors —
doubling over
submitting to her nausea, all she needs
is earthquake angels to ease her
confusion, compulsions stirring
her putrid reflections like ping pong
balls submerged in liquor
submerged in liquor
submerged in liquor.

I ask her to breathe,
but she can't remember how,
and she can't remember why she needs to,
because she knows that once the bus comes
I will be a stranger once again too.

Elmwood

cemetery sunrises soak
weathered feet with temporal
feigned timelessness
foggy plains and bodily remains
echo their desires to gaze out
on the passing days
while I tiptoe
over their stories
when glory days meant survival
dirty knees
and happy mamas

Margins

my thoughts lie
in the margins
to identify
ideas
treated in narrow
disturbed whiteness.
when my ink
crosses the blood
line organ
ization is dis
(e)rupted.
I value
these notes
more than
full pages
trapped in
blank gyres

Green Ink Consultation

Language is a social art —
upside down roads
leading to a catalyst
before you realize
You Are
Catalyst
and God
exists Be
Cause We
Want.

When I Return to the Mountains

Often, I have considered Buddha
presently guiding temporal relativity —
further understanding as greater detachment —
understanding the irony.
Understanding is Irony.
Resurrection is
surface-level reincarnation,
yet temporal relativity still manifests…
Reincarnation is Transference
within another Time. Until
Reincarnation transcends
above surface-level energy,
We Will Know Time. Until
Reincarnation forfeits
death dependency,
We Will Know Life. Until
We forfeit Being,
Speculation Will Be
Our Buddha.

spew

i want to say what's on my mind but know that what's on my mind is grungy and raw and kind of smells like a flower shop with a hint of urine. i want to know i have the power to hurt people and just hurt every one a little bit for a little second, like a pine needle in the ass or a too-hard high five. i want to not live in a limbo of professionalism and agony artistics. i want to create and create and create and create and fuck and create and drink too much coffee and get sweaty and cold. i want to gnaw at the hand of inspiration and spew the chunks that fell off in my mouth. i want to read poetry in the women's restroom and climb as many buildings as i can. i want to pretend to jump off and make everyone suck the air in real quick and intense. i want to make out with a book and get preg nant by swallowing its ideas. i want to birth its baby book and burn it. i want to spread its ashes on my softest parts and let tomorrow swallow me.

I-70

mayhem and lightning
collide like the accident ahead
never sure which causes which
it's all in the timing
it's all in the timing

Flesh Writer

The only difference
between writing on my flesh
and writing on tree flesh
is that mine,
although it has been shredded,
has not been reconstructed into a new,
more fragile substance.
I am shredded much stronger.

Dorm Room Daydreams

I put peacock feathers
through blinds.
When the wind blows,
I like how they fly.

You Never Remember Your Dreams
I Always Remember Mine

Tops of toes kiss,
assuring your presence with me
under blankets too hot,
between dreams too bold —
floppy limbs,
dead senses,
earthly intermission.
I often wonder
if I seep into your dreams
interpersonally —
osmosis from strands
of double-helixed hair
woven between memory
threads in our bed.
I would rather assure
my presence with you,
double-lifed, within
subconscious stressors;
I would rather relieve
you inside there
and dismiss my physicality
as presence right
next to you.

I Love You, Lawrence

Poetry is releasing dead rose petals
out the window while going 90
down the interstate.

Poetry is man eavesdropping on
public transportation.

Poetry is blistered passion.

Poetry is amusement in filling time before death.

Poetry is kissing air and it not kissing you back.

Raw

Rooted in respect
I cower
In fights —
Aren't mine —
Smokesmokedrinksmokedrink
No clean air in between
Just swallowing nasty words
And spitting them right back.
Revert to daydreams and failed
Attempts at reclaiming blood
Stolen from mosquitos.

i follow autopsy pages on the internet

we indulge in tragedy pornography
toofasttoofasttoofast
anticipating and anticipating
          the peak
over.

next?

Just Really Hungry

I saw a man on the corner by the rainbow
cross. He read
Anonymous and propped rusty banjo
memories against pine.
Just really hungry, his cardboard claimed.

Flowers decorated the honest sign, and he ate
one of them roots first.
I did not help.
I did pray for his peace.
The rain came in, and I kept driving.
I did not help.
I did pray for his peace.

existential bull shit

connect the dot freckles
anthropomorphize astronomy,
and the Virgo reveals
Taurus on her leg —
what existential confusion,
what existential bull shit.
Does your palm hold Venus,
because that's what he's been
telling his friends?
The stars are laughing
at you tonight, for you
are not one of them.

family tree

silly putty handprints
look like roots,
and my step-father's stubble
interrupts the line.

I flatten it smooth.

my step-father rolls it
into a rose,
and my step-father hands it back to me.

I flatten it smooth.

my step-father rolls it
into a heart, pats it,
marks it with a B,
and my step-father hands it back to me.

I flatten it smooth.

until the heart is worn
into a hole,
like my step-father's work
genes.

My mother is pregnant,
and my mother cups the putty,
and my mother presses it

against her radiant navel,
and my mother pulls the imprint
into two.
and my mother hands it back to us.
and my step-father hands his piece back to me.
I flatten it smooth.

For Moths and Mothers

Rain pools in my collarbone pocket.
Upon the porch light,
I wish for moth
To drink from me.

Thunder clutches the solitary house,
Gifting it movement that had been
Taken when Warmth chose
Abandonment.

Nature's reverberations don't know
Gentle. Lightning
Envies porch light wishes —
Synthetic bolts for moth's
and mother's comfort.

There are no more stars to wish upon.

Moth's comfort is stolen
For as long as it takes me to sing
Twinkle Twinkle Little Star.

My wish reflects through the pool —
Moth's comfort regained on soggy skin,
Finally drinking from me.

She was too thirsty
To recognize the weight
Of her escape.

She gifts me movement that had been
Taken by my wish.
Wing tip adhered to the nape of my
　　neck,
I collect her soul.

I bow with ease,
Releasing her and spilling
My affiliation.
Her memory will tickle
My collarbone until
The next storm.

to the man who gave me
poetic omnipotence

interactions with
one another
remind me
of pinot noir.
there is a personal
skin of boundary,
but it is thin,
making our cognizance
of one another's depths
fulfill the color
gradation.
once blended,
the outermost ring
of transparency
is enhanced
in our time
together.
if we sip
each other's souls
tomorrow,
it will taste different
than if we indulge
today.

i wish i were a garden

~co-written with kami olson

plant me with the lavender
braid my soft dark petals
between uncut blades
press seedlings into each crease
of my soiled skin

                      wait

                      nourish

                      wait

bury my root-turned toes
to share kisses with worms
and absorb the sky's sorrows

       i   you

         will   will

           grow   wait to harvest me

season by season
let the mood decide my shade
let the bees arouse me
and transfer my soul to the next sprig

Tender Living

I would like to speak to the sky.
It can't help but listen.

Naked in exaggerated light,
I'm illuminated by thoughts of you —
hardened by the bite
and as soft as the hole it makes.

Recurrence

She asked for clarification
as clear as the river
that washed through her thoughts.

Silence…

She asked for knowledge
to cultivate the mighty
and devour the uncertainty.

The sky mumbled
some unmentionables, but
she could not
distinguish which were significant.

Examine your fingers and feel me.

Learn from the voice between stanzas.

Right here we float together.

There's Only One Big Star

little stars in love
form galactic expression —
shapes of our language

Thrift Store Saturdays

glazed loiterers anticipate
clicked on openings
and older women's dedication
without money
we give our time to a god
without money
if I believe in-
tegrity without
a higher cause
am I still a soul
servant with a purpose?
free coffee guides us
through mazes of mismatched dishes
and clothes two sizes too old.
man sings to himself
to His lord
like a character from Dogma
or a fictitious children's bible
while groping ear-
rings' lost stories.
ceramic pigs know tiny hands
loving its insides too excitedly
it shatters
without breaking its gaze.

what have teacups said
because of the lips
that have graced them?
hangover-spoiled breath
craves distractions
offered by a dirty thrift store.

Breaking News

There is a large dissatisfaction
With the way
We represent reality.
No empathy.
Only cheap sentiment.

Z

It's refreshing to be confident
in the energy You emit;
The aura You share
welcomes Me.
Colors commingle,
creating a secondary palette,
without forgetting
Our Primaries.
Zosma may
be a single star,
but Leo wouldn't be complete
without it.
Leo may
be a incandescent lion,
but we must remember
that when a lion shows
its teeth, we cannot assume
it's smiling.

Leo is part of Our galaxy,
and our galaxy is a part of
ten thousand galaxies
measured in the tip of a ballpoint pen.
We are lucky to be
intertwined in all.

Remember...
There is no full moon
in heaven for us
to admire.
To admire
is to recognize
Existence; on this day,
that is You.
Universes are vast,
and today, You made it
noticeably bigger.

Cigarettes and Coffee For Mr. Redding

Embers cascade
From your soulless body,
When you flick your leathered
Fingers.
Splash.
Cold pavement is your canvas
At the bottom of a waterfall of
Contemplation
Depression
Desperation
Desire.
NEED.
Your smoke stories
Penetrate my nostrils
Without asking consent.

Our Commodification of Trees

I)
You steal this peace
of a branch that scarred you, Father,
to show it who's boss of Beauty.

A tree shall not
respect a man;
a man who steals
her week's-worth
color already dies
without him.

Autumn's living
wake gives the wind
one more song before first frost.

You admire her
before you slice
her from core
through dirtied coat.
You admire her
before you convince her
to burn whole.
You admire her
before her remnants
taint your soles.
You admire her
before you burn yourself, too.

II)
I lick this peace
of mahogany memories,
walls of perfectly soft knots,
walls of Grandfather's Home.

Sawdust sweeps through
nostrils moistened
by antiquated cologne
and settles in memory membranes.

Each bud tastes the grain —
grow, my dear.
We shall in this Home.

If walls could talk,
they would cry —
stopping the wind
when it should be
dancing.

If walls could talk,
they would cry
with each stubbed toe,
knuckle to stained surface,
and overbearing containment.

If we talked to walls,
we would cry
in the name of appreciation,
fully knowing
one day we will leave,
and the wind will win,
splinters and nails,
splinters and nails.

They tell me
to remind myself —
create and abandon,
create once more.

III)
We grasp this peace
of knowledge
with, and for,
the power of the world.

From one dead tree
to the next,
We pray for someone
who has written on you
to do more than pray for you.

Wrinkles and roots
strongly and deeply
sap our soul's observations of you.

We caress and prod
recollections between
ground and pressed
slivers of your original form.

Pages are flavored
by our fingerprints;
we wrote
how they tasted homey
but never quite like Home.

We taint you with mismatched ink
bound in animal flesh —
insecurities,
embellished desires,
silent wishes —
always hoping to birth masterpieces.

Ouch

my brain is peeling,
not in a reductive manner,
more
  like
    a snake
          READY FOR GROWTH!
aches of development keep me alive,
until my written words become pins and prick
my pupils with every preposition.

January 11

I only hear
geese moving
toward freedom
        (toward you).
It was dead.

Thanks to
1) oracles
2) fancy language
3) *cool scars*
4) *feelings*

Goodbye, pseudonyms.

We won't miss you.

begging for a different body

please
do not physically and spiritually detach
yourself from this land —
you are working in unity
with the whole body that is Earth.

I once
scraped dirt from plastic trees
I once
asked him
if trees wanted to be
trees
(he said yes)
I once
cried
when I allowed death
to decompose in bed
(the flowers never grew more vibrantly)

I once
wanted
to know what it would be like
to be
a tree
a wind
a puddle

(((growing with every drop)))

(shrinking with every splash)

I once
wanted
to be mad
at wind

until

I once
remembered
I am wind too

[explosion sound]

If you were a poem,
I'd eat you... raw.
Rip you right out
of your freshly printed book
and shove you

as far into my ready mouth
as my tasters and tonsils
and conditioned punching bag allow,
without swallowing you.
I'd marinate you in my saliva
and muster patience
for the slightly soggy,
tender, but still complete,
version of your texture.

I'd grind you down
with my greedy and thorough molars
and get your grated bits
stuck where my wisdom
teeth used to be.

I'd save you

in my gum and cheek pocket,

and every time

I'd pucker my lips,

your words would shoot

tingles across my entire mandible.

Your Real Name is James

For the sake of nostalgia
(mistakes)
and poetic omnipotence

I pray
for someone
to pray
for you

Fitting Into the Fabric of What
These Streets Hold

There's a certain taste to the air
and texture to the people of
the greatest city in the world.

You're right,
everyone should live somewhere
with a lot of colors.

Burgundy time has allowed each Royal gem
to sing louder, more confidently, with more soul,
and for an enthusiastically curious audience.

Men play jazz to dogs and blow kisses
in return for a smile
they've been waiting to incite all day.

Certain boundaries don't exist here,
because the respect of our collective humanity does.

Like Tennessee Williams, I hope to die here,
and part of me will.
I will plant my seed,
because I know the New Orleanians
will love and nurture me properly.

While my seed flourishes here,
the surrounding area of my form from which I
detached it
will die.

I promise to return.

thank you

we fold into fog,
state of coexistence and nonexistence—
all is at peace

Linzi Garcia can be found frolicking through sunflower fields, cemeteries, and bars across the states. She has been featured in *Treading Unique Paths: Young Writers Anthology* (VerbalEyze Press, 2016), *50 Haikus: Issue #12* (Prolific Press, 2017), and on the *Philosophical Idiot* poetry website (November, 2017). If you're lucky, you can even find a haiku of hers in the gumball machine at The Raven Book Store in Lawrence or perhaps hidden in a nook in a tree near you. Linzi currently resides in Lindsborg, Kansas, dreaming of Lawrence Ferlinghetti and New Orleans. She is always looking for invitations to new places where she can absorb new poetry, perspective, incomparable experiences, and quality whiskey.

This project was made possible, in part, by generous support from the Osage Arts Community.

Osage Arts Community provides temporary time, space and support for the creation of new artistic works in a retreat format, serving creative people of all kinds — visual artists, composers, poets, fiction and nonfiction writers. Located on a 152-acre farm in an isolated rural mountainside setting in Central Missouri and bordered by ¾ of a mile of the Gasconade River, OAC provides residencies to those working alone, as well as welcoming collaborative teams, offering living space and workspace in a country environment to emerging and mid-career artists. For more information, visit us at www.oac.com

Osage Arts Community